MW00628003

THE
STUCK
BO🞱K

PICK THIS UP
WHEN YOU DON'T KNOW
WHAT TO DO NEXT

CHRIS
MCALISTER
with Amanda McLeroy

DEDICATION

Dedicated to those who keep believing ...

"There is a season for everything under the sun."

CONTENTS

INTRODUCTION

My daughter recently brought home a giant trophy from her gymnastics studio. This trophy, which is almost as tall as she is, wasn't something she was awarded at a gymnastics meet. This was a team competition trophy that was earned by other gymnasts before she was even on the team. The gym gives away all of their large trophies every few years. Thanks, gymnastics corporate leadership, for de-cluttering your display case while you junk up my house and confuse my daughter about what it means to win. Has it really come to this? Receiving a participation trophy for something in which you weren't even a participant is the height of child sports deception. Never has a trophy held so little meaning, yet provided such a teachable lesson. There is no participation trophy for life. You either perform or you do not. More effort, more time, more hustle, and more trying is not a guarantee to get you unstuck and moving towards the results you want.

Wait a moment. It's easy to be too hard on yourself.

Getting stuck is normal. Acknowledging we're stuck isn't normal because we've invested who we are into our current choices. We've emotionally invested into our decisions by building our identities around our current reality.

We all have places where we are stuck right now. No one has it all together. For those that think they have it all together, a wake up call will eventually appear just as sure as the seasons will change.

We describe the beginning of our wake up using words such as restless, out of sorts, blocked, in a rut, and feeling lost. If the wake up we need is connected to a major part of our lives, we'll use heavier phrases that might include: "something died", "I can't get it back", or "it's over." Maybe we vocalize these frustrations to our co-workers or admit our restlessness to a close friend. Secretly, we might dream of running away from the pressures and responsibilities of life to live on a boat in the Caribbean to escape the pressure of adulting every day.

You had a job you loved and now you have a job you hate. It's the same job you still go to everyday. It's hard to take an honest look at your life and wonder, "Is this as all there is? Is this it?" Maybe you have a degree that you haven't even paid off and it already feels like a prison sentence.

Did you ever think: I could be happy if this one thing would change or a certain person would come into my life or if that certain person would get out of my life?

Instead of taking time to get unstuck, we numb out. We numb out by distracting ourselves from facing reality. Distractions range from alcohol, drugs, social media, shopping, TV, food, community service, to diving in head first into a new hobby or searching for a new love interest. While your distraction of choice might differ from mine, the goal is always the same: to escape the pain and forget about the under-utilized potential of our lives. We know there is something more. Being stuck is our clue.

BEING STUCK ISN'T FAILING

The hardest lesson to learn when you're stuck is actually an "unlearning". The default mode of "try harder, do more" has proven to be fruitless. Time plus effort doesn't always equal the results you want to see. Trying harder and hustling harder will wear you down.

This is why we give up and settle for whatever life throws at us. Convincing ourselves that being stuck is normal, we stop dreaming and growing. This happens because it is easier to go through the motions of life than to acknowledge we are stuck. I don't know who said it but it makes me think of this quote: "Someone once told me the definition of hell: The last day you have on earth, the person you became will meet the person you could have become."

It's not failure to be stuck. Failure is staying stuck. It's growth to recognize and acknowledge we are stuck.

For most people, every area of our life isn't in complete disrepair at the same time. If we divided our lives into basic categories: career, relationships, finances, health, and hobbies, we would notice there are some areas we are stuck while other areas of our lives seem to be working. And we seem to miss the fact that the areas we are stuck in create a spillover effect into the rest of our lives. The entirety of our lives is shaped by what we tolerate or avoid in those stuck areas.

Pause. There is also a place in your life where you are being brilliant. You are so close to seeing fantastic results. We need to learn how to replicate what is working in one area of your life to the other areas you would prefer to ignore. I want to show you how in this book.

WE DON'T NEED MORE INFORMATION

How do we get unstuck? We don't get unstuck by more knowledge or more information. You and I are constantly bombarded with new information every time we turn around. If more knowledge could get us unstuck, we would all be growing more competent and becoming more content each and every day. We would be developing at exponential rates and be healthier and happier than ever. But we aren't. We have the knowledge. We lack the wisdom of situational awareness.

I remember lacking wisdom when I was shopping for an engagement ring for my wife. I wanted to find the perfect ring, but there were so many options that I was stuck trying to make the perfect decision. I assumed that more knowledge would help me get unstuck. I learned everything I could about diamonds. Clarity, color, cut, ratings, settings…I knew what I was looking at and I still couldn't make a decision. Accurately assessing the situation, my dad observed, "The problem is you know too much." I had the knowledge, yet I didn't have the wisdom to make the best decision and relieve the pressure to make the perfect decision.

Never before have there been so many options for every category of our life. Twenty years ago if someone told me they were on a diet; I would have known exactly what they meant. They were simply eating less. If someone said that to me today, I would wonder if they were on a reduced calorie diet, ketogenic diet, or maybe they are only subsisting on cricket protein? There are so many choices. There are an overwhelming number of paths to launch a career and a dizzying amount of ways you could unintentionally end it. You can parent like a helicopter or like a burying beetle that raises her kids inside a corpse (tell your kids to be thankful that isn't your parenting style). Each day presents a new option or fad. This myriad of choices often overwhelms us and we stay stuck.

WHO WE ARE AND WHERE WE ARE

There are two key essential skills to not remain stuck. We need to learn who we are, which I laid out in a previous book at figurethatshiftout.com. Second, we need to know where we are, which is situational awareness. Situational awareness is a skill we need to develop. When we develop this skill to quickly assess where we are and what is next, we'll experience one fantastic result.

We'll have peace. We'll be able to relax. We won't be consumed with wondering, "Am I doing the right thing?" or "Am I taking the right action?" There is no guarantee that what we are doing is going to work, but we relax because we've given ourselves permission to do what is best for us rather than the option we feel pressured to pursue. We can do it our way.

The pathways that we've depended on in previous generations won't be effective as the terrain of the future shifts. Since new pathways are constantly being carved, we learn to take the best action at the best time. We realize in light of all the evidence and all the pathways available, this is the next right step for us.

Situational awareness gives us courage to face what we've tolerated or avoided so we can become unstuck and have the courage to find our own way. We don't engage our lives from a place of fear worried about who we could have become. That initial fear may get us moving, but it won't sustain us. We are sustained by the joy of finding our own way.

WHERE ARE YOU?

This book gives you a mental model to the second critical component for making decisions: learning where you are. We can learn to quickly assess where we are right now in specific areas of our lives and take the wise path moving forward. Most of us were never taught how to assess where we are and how to decide for ourselves what was the wise path. Instead we were exposed to the subtle pressure of the expected path of our traditions or the aggressive pressure from the authoritarian voices of our upbringing. Some of us grew up hearing pop psychology that told us to only say good things and everything would work out. If we learned the secret of how to attract the results we want, then whatever it was would magically appear and we would all live happily ever after. If life were that easy, then everyone would choose the right path every time. As a result, you and I would automatically live the life we wanted without effort.

Wisdom is looking at where we are and assessing what the best action is to get you on your right path. Wisdom gives us the courage to admit that the path that was right last year isn't the path that is going to help us grow stronger and healthier. Wisdom is acknowledging that I am stuck in between a tension of what worked yesterday and what is no longer working today. This tension of two realities blocks my ability to take the next step on my path. I have to release what worked and embrace the uncertainty of what might or might not work. The goal is to change our awareness and reframe our mindset to help us accurately assess faster and recover more quickly. The model offered in the following pages isn't a discovery of what is new; it is a rediscovery of what is true.

CHAPTER 1:
LOOKING FOR SOLID GROUND

Getting unstuck will require finding your own path. Finding your own path isn't about being rebellious and trying to assert your will for your own validation. It's a rejection of the traditions and expectations that no longer serve you in your path. You and I aren't thumbing our nose at the previous generation. We aren't trying to demand our independence while we stomp our feet like a toddler and say, "You're not the boss of me." Instead, we gratefully acknowledge the people before us did the best they could with what they thought they should do. We will use some of their wisdom, but also have the courage to acquire some of our own. We are going to become mapmakers.

Learning the art of becoming a mapmaker is essential because the maps of yesterday aren't enough. They are no longer helpful in the increasing complexity of a constantly changing terrain. Imagine what it was like to plan a road trip from Montana to Florida fifty years ago. Someone would pull out a piece of paper that was folded up like an accordion. The driver would carefully open the map up so it wouldn't rip. Then, the navigator would trace an imaginary line from Montana to Florida memorizing which interstates were on the route and which towns or cities would be the best option to pull off the interstate each night. Your family would drive from hotel to hotel trying to find an available room.

Imagine how you and I would take that same road trip today. We would plan out our route, but we wouldn't use the $4.99 folded map sold at gas stations. Instead of spending hours listening to the kids in the back seat begging to stop at a hotel with a pool, most of us would make a reservation in advance on our computer or phone only after we checked the hotel's reviews and accommodations. Then, using the hotel's app on our phone, we could cancel our reservation or change reservations at any point along the way. What is a road trip without traffic? There are apps on our phones that alert us to wrecks, heavy traffic and delays so we are constantly able to change roads to avoid traffic. Is it wrong to plan our road trips differently than our parents and grandparents? Looking at these changes, we can see that in many ways, we have already become a new generation of mapmakers.

WE NEED A MODEL TO GET US GOING

How can we become mapmakers for ourselves? We
need a meta-model, a model that is vast enough to be
timeless and robust enough to be individualized. We
need a model to provide a quick situational awareness
of where we are in the complexity of so many options,
but still allow a nuanced approach for the particularity
our situation. We want to develop the skill of getting a
quick macro view of our lives and figuring out the next
micro step. Instead of just seeing the forest or the
trees, we want to see the forest and notice the trees.
We need to be able to look at our situations and
problems and then orient on our map based on this
new information. This skill will allow us to be more
aware, to sequence better options faster, and to
recover from challenges more efficiently. This quick
mental ordering and orientation allows us to be
resilient amidst the complexity of life.

Before we get into the model that I'm offering you in
the following chapter, I want to set the groundwork
for why this model is so critical. To understand why
you and I need this model, let's look at how
transportation changed in the early 1900's and notice
how it is changing today.

It is easy to be stuck and not see the changes that are
coming. Most changes build slowly, and then they sweep in
quickly. If you drive a truck for a living, you are in a job that
is going to be phased out. It will be phased out by trucks
that drive themselves. Your skill set is not going to be

needed at some point in the future. People can hear that but they don't actually prepare for the coming changes. They just keep repeating the same actions they repeated the day before.

Think about what it was like to own a company that dispatched horse and buggies around town in the late 1800's. How comfortable was the person who owned a successful business maintaining and repairing the buggies? Would you have felt financially secure if your job was shoeing horses? Would you have felt threatened by the invention of the automobile or would you have dismissed the idea? How many people did not adjust to the industry changes and found themselves out of a job years later? These people were phased out. Their skill set became obsolete.

It's a trippy thought to think that families could have noticed and prepared for these changes. Imagine parents sitting around the dinner table with their children saying, "Some day you will not ride horses around town. You'll drive cars." That probably didn't happen too often because most people are in the moment, copying what they did yesterday, just repeating today. They are stuck.

People need to be able to make their own map instead of following the map that is handed down to them. Imagine a father saying, "You should get a job driving a truck because I drive a truck. I was able to save money in my 20's by sleeping in the truck and not wasting money on rent. Today, I own my truck and make a good living driving it." If the son wants to make his father happy, he might stuff his own dreams and desires and reply, "Yes, I will use your map and follow your path." The son will soon find himself stuck since he will follow a map that was never meant to be his.

Mapmakers have learned how to anticipate not just cultural change, but more importantly, the personal change needed in their lives. This awareness allows us to be prepared for what is next. We don't let the fear of someone judging our decisions keep us stuck. We learn to take the best actions at the right moment and realize that sometimes the best action is to patiently wait for better timing. We learn to live our lives with situational awareness. Without situational awareness, most people react by powering up or shrinking back. Some people power up to a difficult situation by trying to seize control of a situation. This is done when we use yelling, physical threats, body language, and harsh language as shock and awe tactics to overwhelm anyone or any situation we view as a threat. The second reaction occurs when we shrink back and cower quietly without a voice. This happens when we accept being knocked down because we don't know how to respond or when we passively accept what the world has thrown at us. Either response leaves us stuck. Take a moment to imagine addressing a situation at hand with the right action, the right intensity, and then having the courage to stand behind your reaction to move forward.

I CAN'T CONTROL WHAT YOU THINK OF ME

How much of our stuckness is related to worrying about what others will think of our choices? No matter what actions or steps we take, someone will judge us. They might even misunderstand us and try to stop us. Courage is required when we take authentic actions. We have to release this false idea that we can control what others think of us; it's our life. We aren't trying to gain control of our lives from someone else and tell the rest of the world their viewpoint doesn't matter. This isn't about a fight. It's about a reframing. We start to look at our situations through a different filter. Rather than our lives being about, "What will they think?" we filter our decisions through, "Where am I and what do I need to do?" Our lives become our own gift to open.

We learn to be present with our lives rather than distracted. We do this by making our own map. If we make a map based on what we wished our lives looked like or what we think others expect from us, our map is useless. It's a fake map with fake names and fake Interstates. With social media posts and a few well-edited pictures, we can make our lives look healthy and happy. We can show the world a fake map that we would like to believe. A good mapmaker looks at the terrain and acknowledges both the mountains and the valleys.

HAPPY AND CRAPPY

A number of years ago I learned about a simple way of checking in with others that I used with our family at dinner. The question was "Has anything made you sad, mad, or glad?" This shortened into a version that became, "Any highs or lows you'd like to share?" Eventually, I passed this on in a college lecture. Those college students changed my wording slightly. Now I ask, "Any happies or crappies to share?"

We need to know where we are with friends, where we are with family, where we are with business, where we are in our spirituality, where we are in our health, our hobbies and any part of life that makes us feel happy or crappy. We ask ourselves about our happies and crappies to be present. We need to learn how to be present with our lives. Being present makes us grateful for what we have and shows us areas that might need change. Being present means we acknowledge what is good and what is bad for us rather than using someone else's map.

Change happens. Hard seasons happen. Surprises happen. They blindside us and leave us gasping for air. Imagine getting knocked down for a moment and then being able to look at our own map to decide how to react. Our mapmaking provides a course of action. It shows us what area we need to change so we stop taking the worst actions that keep us on a path that isn't working. When we get knocked down we don't stay disoriented, instead we gain orientation. We can relax before we see the results we want to see.

CHECK YOURSELF BEFORE YOU WRECK YOURSELF

The worst approach you can take when you're stuck is to try harder or hustle harder. It saps your joy and keeps you from getting the life you want. The illusion of you-can-have-what-you-want-if-you-try-hard-enough is a dangling carrot that will always remain out of your reach.

I'm tired of hearing about hustle. Most people translate hustle into "do more with more intensity". It's as useless as a dog chasing its tail or a hamster running on the wheel. Hamsters…dogs…I've got all the cliché metaphors you need. Clichés stick around because they are true.

Hustle harder for enough time and you'll turn into a panicked leader. Panicked leaders repeat approaches that stress the people around them.

The crazy truth is that being able to relax under pressure will deliver everything people have been trying to accomplish with the "try harder" or "hustle harder" approach.

Can you relax under the pressure? This is how you check in with yourself before you wreck yourself and take out those closest to you.

Relaxing in the pressure delivers these benefits:

Relaxing reminds you that you are more than your work and business.

It's easy to start to confuse who you are with your role. This creates undue amounts of anxiety. Anxious leaders create anxious followers. Anxious followers wreck your best intentions. It's like a road trip that should be a blast but keeps getting hijacked by the annoying behaviors of the unaware.

Relaxing facilitates creative breakthroughs. Release the problem while you relax, but hold it in the margin of your mind. The creative solutions will arrive. Rather than seeing either/or solutions, you'll start to see both/and solutions. Rather than worry about being passed by those you feel you're competing with, you'll leapfrog over them with your insights.

Relaxing protects you from forcing decisions. When a decision is creating anxiety, it might be that you need the creative breakthrough. You'll also need an honesty session with yourself. Relaxing helps you stop the BS. The truth surfaces and you stop hyping yourself with, "I should want _____." Or you deceive yourself by saying, "I shouldn't want _____." Who says? Be honest about what you really want and then commit to your decision even when you are uncertain. Free yourself of the "shoulds" and the "should nots".

Relaxing helps you make a decision. It's normal to feel confused at moments. As options and responsibilities increase there is a complexity that can drain your brain causing you to shut down. Lead others? Own a business? Start a committed relationship? Become a parent? Need to pick a major? Change your business model? Taking on more responsibilities can increase your stress if you pressure yourself to make perfect decisions. Relaxing is living in the freedom that your identity isn't at stake with every decision.

Relaxing improves your approach. Those who hustle harder don't always work smarter. Relaxed leaders find the best ways to unblock their motivation and the motivation of others. Uptight and insecure leaders try to keep themselves and others hyped up.

Relaxing grows your ability to reach clarity. You can't strive your way into clarity. You relax into clarity. A relaxed state of mind is not a distracted mind. It is clear. It is focused on what is intended. Once you're clear on your intentions, then you have achieved clarity. Leaders who can't relax experience diminishing returns for their efforts because they do not have clarity so they cannot focus.

Relaxing won't make you lazy. I'll acknowledge that people tend to be sloppy at the edges of anything they are executing. But you don't have to be uptight. Relaxing increases your speed of insight. The insight renews you and your courage. Rather than feeling stressed and getting sloppy, you take that gift of energy and allow it to help you finish tasks well.

Relaxing won't cause you to lose your edge. You'll sharpen your edge. Relaxing doesn't mean you're indifferent. You'll still care. You'll still be dedicated. Leading people carries a specific loneliness to it and can hollow you out over time. Learning to refill is not only enjoyable; it is necessary. Those advanced at relaxing learn how to deepen their capacity while they refill it. Figure out the activities and places that help you feel so relaxed you can exclaim to yourself, "It's going to be OK." And then have fun practicing.

I spent my 20s afraid that I was getting passed by the accomplishments of others. I couldn't relax in the pursuit of my goals because I was convinced I was running out of time. Even when I accomplished big things, I still couldn't relax since it was never enough. I finally learned to relax during a financial crisis when I went from a multi-million-dollar project to near bankruptcy. Afterwards, as I sat staring at an eviction notice, I began to realize I could relax even in the midst of great loss and misfortune. I learned to relax in the midst of the pressure instead of waiting for life to be perfect. I took naps in the sun. I accomplished my goals. I got back on my feet by decreasing the intensity of my hustle and increasing the clarity of it. I stopped increasing the pressure I put on myself.

Relaxing doesn't require a weeklong retreat. You can recover on the run. You don't have to get away for a week or even a weekend. It requires no money or tech.

Relaxing makes you a better human. Rather than anxiously hustling all the time, you learn to appreciate the simple beauty of the moment. You can be present. You can change your mind. You can laugh at yourself and your mistakes. You are more gracious with your struggles. Grace to yourself will naturally overflow to others. You can harness the ability to relax those around you. There is no one you are connected to who wants to receive any less grace from you.

Relaxing teaches you the ultimate reality: Another accomplishment or pursuit or measurement will not make you happy. Learning to be happy where you are is the ultimate mindset. Relaxing is how you begin to defeat the fear of messing up and missing out. No longer worried about being passed by you start to relax and let your foot off the gas. Clarity emerges out of peace.

Relaxing helps you become the kind of leader the world needs right now.

Relaxing brings you back to center of knowing who you are and where you are.

Getting unstuck is about making the best decision knowing where we are. Situational awareness helps us relax.

THE MODEL THAT HAS ALWAYS BEEN THERE

The model we are going to use to gain situational awareness is to think about our lives through the lens or filter of the seasons. To understand this filter experientially we need to think of ourselves as a tree. We are going to look at the tree as it goes through four distinct seasons: fall, winter, spring and summer. Just like the tree can't control the seasons in nature, we are going to acknowledge there are many areas of our life that we cannot control. A tree doesn't get mad when its leaves are gone, its branches are bare, and there is a layer of snow all over it. Instead of anger or frustration, the tree uses that season to prepare for spring buds, summer droughts and fall insect infestations. The tree teaches us: we don't control the seasons, but we can cooperate with them.

Generalized wisdom becomes customized wisdom based on which season you are in at this moment. The actions you take will be nuanced actions based on which season of life you are in at the moment and what is the best action for your best future. You will learn to apply this truth: you are only stuck when you fail to cooperate with the seasons.

CHAPTER 2:
FALL

While out on a date with my wife, we had a chance to try a new apple dessert that one of our favorite restaurants was introducing. I love any dessert with apples so I could not wait to try it. During dinner, all I wanted to eat was the caramel apple cake topped with a scoop of ice cream that our server had mentioned. Finally, another server brought our dessert to the table and I dove in. It was so good! I couldn't quite put my finger on what tasted different about the cake. It was delicious. I even told my wife, "I don't know what they did, but this is the best apple cake I've ever eaten!" Our server happened to walk up to our table just as I was going on and on about the apple cake. She started laughing as she explained the other server had brought us a caramel blondie with a scoop of ice cream. I was sitting at the table raving about an apple desert that didn't have a single apple. Our mind can convince us of something that isn't true. And it's happening to us all the time.

Change begins in the fall season. It is here we start noticing the ways that we are tricking ourselves. The fall season is when you and I finally realize we do not have control over as much as we like to believe. We stop tricking ourselves about reality. We become aware of reality. And then we accept it.

The fall season is a wake up call to our potential. There's a gap to close. The gap is between where we are and where we want to be. That gap won't close by doing what you did yesterday or today. Trying harder, forcing it, yelling more, or whatever strategy we refuse to release will keep us stuck in the fall. We will stay mentally deceived by tricking ourselves.

Superstitions like rain dances were once common because people thought, "If we dance for the gods, they will be happy and provide rain for our crops." I can sympathize with how it began. Thousands of years ago a farmer faced a daunting and uncontrollable situation anytime drought conditions were affecting his crops. He needed rain so his fields would produce and he would be able to feed his family. I can imagine under that pressure when the crops were about to die, he mentally lost it and danced in desperation in his field. He couldn't look at a radar and see rain coming. He danced. It rained. He connected the dots in false way. What was a breakdown became a superstition.

You and I may not believe in rain dances, but have you ever thought, "If I do this one thing, it's going to make everything work." In college I knew a girl who would drive onto campus saying, "If there is a parking spot in the front parking lot, I'll go to class. If not, it's a sign to go back home." I'll let you guess how long it took her to flunk out and move back home. From an apple cake to our rain dances, it's time to stop tricking ourselves.

AWARE OF REALITY

We have utilized modern day technology to gain a false sense of control. We place surveillance cameras around our homes, put alarms on our cars, track our kids' cell phones, and take self-defense classes as if these measures will guarantee control over our lives and possessions. The illusion of control can vanish in a moment. We need the fall to wake us up to the wisdom to know the difference between what we can change and control and everything beyond our control. Our change process begins when we face reality and acknowledge we control very little.

It's a common experience to have a day when you feel like everything is going as planned and then a single phone call, email or conversation throws your day, your bank account balance or a relationship spiraling out of control. This is why so many people live in fear "waiting for the other shoe to drop". Yet the very moment our world turns upside down can be an opportunity to choose to numb out or wake up.

The wake up doesn't have to begin with dramatic moments. Fall seasons can begin anytime we realize we have ourselves trapped. We might notice that we continue to set higher and higher goals thinking at some point we will achieve control and peace. Maybe the goal for our business is to finally hit six figures. Once we hit six figures, we realize that amount of money didn't solve all of our problems. We immediately set a higher goal hoping it will fix our old problems as well as the new issues that emerged when our business grew. Months later we are further down the same road with the same issues, but now we realize we are also short staffed. Where is the control we were supposed to have once we "made it"? Six figures, half a million, one million, five million… Are you and I playing the role of Dr. Evil in an *Austin Powers* movie, displaying our need for power and control by holding everyone around us ransom for one hundred billion dollars? Like Dr. Evil, we have no idea what one hundred billion dollars looks like, but how do we back down? Pressing in harder to control something when it's broken is a response of someone stuck in a fall season.

ACCEPTING REALITY

The fall season is doing it's work in us the moment we start to let go of our false control and forced activities. We are failing the test of the fall season when we stay committed to strategies that aren't working. We need to release something instead of trying to redouble our efforts.

I use questions to help me accept reality in the fall season. The questions are easy to ask, but tough to answer because we have to stop lying to ourselves and stop ignoring the signs. When I started losing my hair and going bald I tried to prop up a false reality. Accepting reality meant Mario

Lopez couldn't be my hair idol. It had to now be Matt Lauer.

Here are some questions I ask myself to help me accept and face reality: "Where am I frustrated? Where am I worried? What gets under my skin too quickly? When do I react with a level ten response to a level two problem? When am I tired? Where could there be a better result? Where am I forcing something?" These questions can cut through our fake reality when we honestly evaluate where we are today. What questions could you add to this list?

Truth > Hyped Positivity

The test to pass in the fall season is to value truth over a hyped positivity. Truth is greater than hyped positivity. Once we learn to accept reality, then we can be positive about the growth that is possible. In the 9th grade, I had a blast playing basketball, street hoops style with my friends. Anytime I felt tired I would tell myself, "I'm big, I'm strong, I'm tall, and have lots of energy." My self-talk was my way of keeping my street game on point. I tried out for the school team. I was confident I'd make the team because I had been telling myself that I was big, strong, tall, and I have lots of energy. While my friends and I were waiting for the roster to be posted, the coach pulled me aside and said, "Hey, we need some help. Do you want to be the team manager?"

I wanted to play. I didn't want to keep stats. Being in the game is where the action is and being the team manager felt too passive. The problem was I hadn't hit my growth spurt in 9th grade, so I was one of the shorter guys. There was no amount of hyping my mental state that could make me tall enough and strong enough to make the team. I had to let go of my fantasy and accept reality. Remember our statement for fall: Truth > Hyped Positivity.

This is why I think a lot of self-help is vacuous and unhelpful. Truth is greater than hyped positivity. We want to grow, but it's not going to happen until we accept the reality of where we are in this moment. At one point in my early 30s, I had a massive six-figure debt from a bad business decision. I did not want to acknowledge these facts. As I would drive down the road, I would occasionally say it out loud to help myself accept the situation so I could eventually change it.

The fall season is an opportunity for change. We accept reality so we can stop pursuing fantasies that won't change our future. The relationship is over. The business failed. The idea didn't work. Fall means it's time for some leaves to drop to the ground.

I have a funny visual I use in my head when I'm stuck in a fall season. I imagine myself trying to staple, tape, and pin leaves back onto a tree branch. It sounds silly but it helps me become aware and accept my current circumstance.

Even if you and I taped hundreds of dead orange and red speckled leaves back onto the tree branches in October, what would it accomplish? How long could we pretend the leaves hadn't died? How long would we walk around complaining that the tree 'shouldn't' have lost its leaves? If we won't yell at a tree because it dropped its leaves in fall, why can't we be kind to ourselves to let those leaves fall? Everything we need to let go of may have been life giving at one time, but it's time for change.

Fall is the death season. It is when we learn to let go of what isn't working. Letting go allows us to move through the fall season and not stay stuck. These actions will help us progress to the winter season and take that next step of growth.

Action #1: Stare down what you want to ignore.

If we are avoiding reality, we are going to stay stuck. I want to continually grow and develop. It makes me sad to see how many people become worse versions of themselves as they age. The beginning point to a lifetime of growth is to honestly look at what you'd like to avoid. At any given moment in our lives, we all have places like this. No one stands on a perfectly secure pedestal. No life is as solid as it seems. Healthy people learn to address the next area of growth as they become aware of it.

The next area of growth could be a part of life that needs to turn around. It could also be a part of life that needs to stop coasting. The fall is a moment to look at the bad or the best and know, "It can be better." In no category of my life would I assess that last year's results were good enough. I

want my relationships with friends and family to continue
to improve throughout my lifetime.

Action #2: Learn the difference between a path and a destination.

There will be pain when we face reality. But hope can be
accessed and cultivated when we learn the difference
between a path and a destination. As I type this, I'm
dreaming of a beach vacation with my family this summer. I
also have the estimate the orthodontist handed my wife for
the cost of my daughter's braces. The destination is the
beach and the braces are blocking the path. I can accept
that the path changed. Paths do change. The braces will
mean more to her in the long term than a beach vacation.
Distinguishing between the path and destination helps me
see other paths to the destination. We may still make it to
the beach this summer. We may not. The fall season might
change our destination or it might require us to change our
path.

One way of identifying the fall season is to decide if we are
running from something instead of running to something.
The fall season is an invitation to let go of old attachments,
to shed old leaves. When we develop attachments to our
paths and lose sight of our destination, it is easy to develop
addictions. These addictions keep us distracted. Being
distracted will keep us in the fall season. Distractions allow
us to continue to lie to ourselves and remain on the wrong
path.

While working on this book, we noticed (and by "we" I mean my wife) a funny smell coming out of the laundry room. This unique scent wasn't our sweaty gym clothes. Apparently my wife thinks a burning chemical smell is a cause to be alarmed. Upon inspection, I found the hot water hose was scalding hot. The melting rubber hose was giving off a putrid smell. The washer had stopped using cold water and was only flowing with molten lava. Most of the time when stuff like this comes up I know I'm out of my league, but I thought I'd give it a try.

A quick internet search helped me find the part I needed to order. I paid extra for quick shipping and waited patiently. The part came in and I began the surgery. I had to watch a few videos online to figure out how to get the back panel off. By the time I found the damaged part, I was already dripping sweat. I started to get the back panel on when the hose attachment dropped behind the panel. This meant I had to take the panel off, again.

I already had one extra screw that wouldn't fit anywhere. After I secured the panel for the second time, I had two extra screws leftover. Once I attached the hoses to the wall, I realized I had mixed up the hot and cold hose. Then as I started switching the hoses, the attachment piece fell behind the panel again! I had to take the panel off a third time! Finally the hoses were attached. Cold water was flowing. We were back.

I told one of my daughters to cue up the new "Be humble" rap song. Of course, I would have also taken the "I'm the man" song. As my wife watched, I set the washer to start a cycle and listened as the cold water filled the tub. Then, there was silence. No movement. No spinning. Nothing. I had broken the washer. I was so mad and frustrated. I had exhausted time, energy and money with absolutely nothing to show for it.

The path was "this washing machine needs to work". The next day, I bought a new machine. The destination was a washing machine that worked. I had to release the path that wasn't working. Releasing a path isn't easy. In the past, stuff like this would cause me to be tense and uptight with those around me. While I did punch the machine in my mind, I didn't actually punch it and that felt like growth. Just to check on myself I asked my wife how she thought I had handled the situation. I said, "If 10 is a mess and 1 is awesome then how'd I do?" She said, "I only heard a couple f-bombs, I'll give you a 3."

Action #3: Acknowledge what isn't working.

In the fall we let go of what isn't working. We have to accept our current circumstances before we can know how to improve them. You know the conversation you want to have with your partner, but you keep using the same ineffective approach. Later, after you have both insecurely hurt each other, you question the value of the relationship rather than acknowledging the inadequacy of your approach. Getting underneath the surface of an issue demands we have to be present, aware, and honest. We want to shed and release any false hype or 'shoulds' that have us stuck.

If we stay in the fall season too long, we will create storms and chaos based on the false ideas we have accepted as truth. Whatever chaos and pain we are facing in a fall season can and probably will get worse if we continue to ignore what isn't working. False truths will not take us to the next level.

Years ago when my kids were upgrading from crib beds to "big girl beds", I had a problem with one bolt or screw or whatever...I hate handyman stuff as you might have noticed.

After assembling the entire bed, I had a bolt that was supposed to attach the bed frame to the headboard, and it stuck out three inches. When I'd try to push the headboard against the wall, it would scratch the drywall. If it was pushed hard enough, it was going to puncture a hole in the drywall. I needed a shorter bolt!

I ran to the local hardware store and described the problem to the helpful gentleman in aisle 17. I asked for a shorter bolt that was the same size or if he had a machine he could use to cut this bolt down to the size I needed. A knowing smile crept across his face as I described the problem. In one swift motion, he reached over to the bolt I was holding and flipped it to face the other direction. AHHHH!

In other words, the bolt was fine, I just needed to flip the direction of the long end. The long end of the bolt was designed to go towards the bed frame. I could try harder all I wanted, but until I flipped the bolt I was going to keep getting the same result. I could watch home improvement videos and get hyped while slamming a red bull, yet I still had to flip the direction of the bolt. A small directional change was what I needed.

We go hard at our problems thinking more intensity will help. It won't.

We start to take our results personally and think something must be wrong with us.

You're not the problem. It's your approach.

It's the stubborn commitment to a wrong direction that's holding you back.

Think of one idea, action, principle, metaphor, or analogy that you are holding onto that is keeping you stuck. It may have served you well in the past, but it is keeping you stuck today. Transitioning into the next season will not occur if we force a path that needs to be abandoned. What area is broken that you have yet to face with authenticity?

There will be new actions, principles and metaphors to guide us. The chaos and pain will birth new dreams and renew some of our old ones. That's getting ahead of where the seasons will take us next. Before we move into the new, we go deeper into reality as we enter the winter. We don't have to waste our time with superstitious rain dances and we won't be tricked by blondies disguised as apple cake.

*

CHAPTER 3:
WINTER

One winter my wife noticed a leak under our sink. She had
kept an eye on it throughout the day and realized it was
quickly becoming a big problem. When I walked in that
night, she showed me the leak. It was early December and
the timing felt awful. Christmas is expensive and I didn't
want to fork over cash for this annoying problem. I decided
to patch the leak and deal with the real issue after the
Christmas rush had died down. I went to the hardware
store and told the sales clerk my problem. I shared my plan
to buy silicon spray and seal the area around the faucet
connector that was leaking. Looking for his buy-in I asked,
"What do you think?" I don't know if he had seen the
commercials on TV advertising the hyped up silicon spray
that was advertised to stop any leak, too. Maybe he didn't
have a clue how to fix a leaking faucet so agreeing with me

was his easiest answer. Regardless, he approved my plan and I went home to save the day.

For the record, it worked. I was the hero, the man, Mr. Fix-It. Well, that's what I felt like as I walked around our kitchen feeling like I deserved my own home improvement show on PBS. And again, for the record, I had stopped the leak under the sink. Fast forward to a few days before Christmas. As I walked into the basement one evening, I noticed water trickling down the basement wall and forming a puddle on the floor. Recognizing this problem had gone from bad to worse, I called a plumber. To add salt to my wound, it was after eight o'clock so I knew I was going to pay the after hours rate.

He confirmed what I knew. The faucet was ruined and we needed a new one. He just happened to have a $500 designer faucet with him. Unfortunately, it didn't match our kitchen. He offered to install a less expensive faucet if I could buy one while he waited at my house, but it was late and the stores were already closed. My little leak problem turned into an expensive problem because I forced something that wasn't working.

In the winter season, the action that keeps you stuck is to frantically try anything and everything. The winter is a moment to stop and be still so we can investigate. The temptation is to hurriedly escape the thing that we noticed wasn't working in the fall season. We look like a wild animal trying to claw our way out of a cage when we are desperate to avoid the winter season. We hustle with an ineffective approach. We feel isolated. In that isolation we return to old reactions to force a change. Not many of us want the winter season, but let's look at the tree and see why it needs the winter.

During the winter, a tree extends and expands its root system, searching for nutrients and water that it will utilize in the spring season. Winter is also necessary to preserve and strengthen the tree itself. During our winter, we will give ourselves permission to stop what isn't working so we can grow stronger. As we'll learn, stopping doesn't mean walking out on our relationship or quitting our job tomorrow. Instead, we give ourselves permission to grieve what was lost or stolen. How do we face a winter season? We lean in. We explore the reality we learned to accept in fall. We study how, why, and what happened that made us stuck.

Here is our breakthrough for the winter season: When we want to increase the intensity by desperately trying to escape the season, we actually need an increase in clarity.

Clarity > Intensity

When I work with companies and teams, I always know when someone is stuck in fall/winter transition because they will try to make up for their lack of clarity with an increase of intensity. They don't know what isn't working and why it isn't working so they hide behind intensity. Have you ever sat in that meeting? The leader rants and rails against every report, every suggestion, and everybody. They will say out loud or communicate with their body, "This isn't what I wanted." They fail to honestly admit, "I don't know what I want, but this isn't it." The leader doesn't know what he wants or what would solve the problem, but he is too insecure to own it. Instead, he lashes out at anyone who dares to raise his or her head out of the foxhole.

Intensity isn't always displayed as a negative lashing out against others. Intensity can also be a hyped distraction. I like to imagine Tom Brady's mechanics coach in his face yelling, "Do you want to win another Super Bowl?" Of course he does. Hyping him to state an obvious commitment is intensity. I know little about football but clarity would be his mechanics coach saying, "When you throw past 20 yards you hold the ball with your pinky too far out and lose some speed." That is clarity. Again I am imagining this based on my little understanding, but the analogy holds true. Winter is working when you start noticing the lashing out or the hyping up as a way of attempting to manufacture a response.

How do we reach that clarity? The winter season assists us. The core question for winter is, **"Why isn't it working?"** Remember the fall core question is, "Why is this happening to me?" so you can see the progression of growth the seasons facilitate. In the fall we identified the problem or the rut that we could no longer ignore. We didn't try to fix it. We noticed it. We owned it. But now in the winter season, we have core work to do. Just like a tree does in winter, when it looks like the trunk is dead and the branches are barren, the core is being strengthened. In our winter we are being strengthened. We have to sit still in the cold, blowing wind and study what is going on around us and in us. Most of us are ready to leave the winter season the moment we face it. There is suffering and sadness in the winter. If we refuse to face the winter season, we will stay stuck in that area of our life and risk it spilling over into other areas of our life. We risk walking away before we are ready to face the next season.

The flip side is staying in winter too long. Have you ever known someone who refused to leave the winter season? You can recognize them because they are often bitter, angry and resentful. Instead of facing the season, even if it was 100% unfair, they stay in winter afraid of releasing the hurt and blame. We wreak havoc on ourselves and everyone around us when we fail to navigate a winter season.

We have two extremes to avoid. We don't obsess over the pain of our winter nor do we fail to acknowledge what hurts. We don't build an igloo to live in our winter permanently. And we don't force a fake smile when our arm has been cut off and we're bleeding out. How do we do this? We continue asking the question, "Why isn't this working?" When we want to quit, we lean in. We keep examining.

The answers you find to the questions may sound different on day five than it did the first hour you noticed what was not working. Sometimes you are not ready to accept the next step. Other times you might actually pinpoint the true problem in a matter of minutes. Some issues are so complex and painful that it may take longer to admit or even realize the core issue.

Leaning in means we are present. We pay attention. We notice actions and reactions. We freely give compassion and acceptance to ourselves in the midst of our struggle.

Winter season is not the time to lecture yourself with, "You knew better. How did you not see it coming? You deserve this." That shame keeps you stuck. It isn't healthy and it isn't helpful.

Getting unstuck in any season requires action. Those actions are different for each season. The winter season can trick you because the action required develops your mindset. The winter reveals where your mindset is weak and fragile. This is what makes the process of the winter season difficult for many of the ambitious leader types I work with. The pain of the winter makes you desperate to do whatever is necessary to relieve your pain. Stay in the moment of your pain as you reflect. You're not cooperating with your winter unless you see what you have not been able to see. I know the winter is cold and it hurts. The natural impulse to escape this moment means you will try to find the least uncomfortable way to end the winter season by returning to the familiarity of the fall. The new activity of the spring will feel unfamiliar and different but it's a better feeling than the darkness of the winter. Explore the cave of your winter. You can't hype yourself to the light of spring. Let it break forth by feeling the weight of this moment without running away.

This season tends to favor the introvert who enjoys thinking and analyzing. Even if you prefer a more extroverted approach of action, you will have to cooperate with what this season is developing in you to become whole. Three actions will help you cooperate with the winter as it sharpens the weak parts of your mindset.

Action #1: Stop the self-sabotage of ineffective hustle.

In a winter season the false belief that hustle will fix everything shows up in an obvious way if we slow down enough to notice it. Ineffective hustle happens because you believe others are passing you by and if you let up on the gas, you'll get left behind.

I think of this obvious behavior through the lens of a road trip. If you're the leader of the road trip, imagine you are the driver and everyone on your team is in the car. I want to help you learn to recognize your behavior and the behavior of others. The following ineffective behaviors will ruin the road trip:

The 8 Personalities of an Ineffective Hustle.

Personality 1: The Forced Smiler

Mode of operation: "Afraid to rock the trip's itinerary."

Convinced that conflict means bad things, they sacrifice forward movement for forced calm. This person is afraid to turn the spotlight onto themselves when their strengths are needed. Because of this, the people on the road trip miss out on their contribution and the Forced Smiler doesn't ask for what they need. They might need to pee, but won't ask you to stop and then they will blame you for not stopping when they are desperate.

Personality 2: The Humble-Bragger

Mode of operation: "Look who I'm in the car with! Wooo!"

They are less concerned with moving the journey forward and helping the team win. Being seen in the right car with the right people is extremely important to this person. Bragging about who they hang with is their telltale sign. Concerned they might be kicked out of the road trip; they stay consumed with fitting in and constantly manipulate people and situations for a better position.

Personality 3: The Menacer

Mode of operation: "Disturbs the trip to keep power."

Right when things are going well, the Menacer throws a wrench in the trip to comfort themselves with their power. They flash with aggression, forced conflict, and sometimes violence. Afraid to deeply commit to a team and give up their preferred agenda to the group agenda, they keep others at a distance and their status of power known.

Personality 4: The Brow Furrower

Mode of operation: "Quiet in the corner."

Void stares and expressionless mannerisms make them seem copacetic. But it's just a cover-up to keep from getting called on to contribute. What they really feel is, "I don't want to screw this up." Their quiet isn't good. They have some special strength that the road trip and its people need. When they get called on to help their brow furrows in pain as they anxiously fear messing up.

Personality 5: The Crisis Maker

Mode of operation: "Lights fires in the backseat."

Convinced they are only needed on the team if there is a fire to put out, they keep the entire team in a state of chaos as they continue to light fires. The Crisis Maker complains about the fire while the hot match burns out behind their back. The crisis maker is unaware that messes of their own making activate them. Unfortunately, the seat cushions can only be patched so many times before they are destroyed.

Personality 6: The Squirrel Chaser

Mode of operation: "Makes sharp unannounced turns."

The Squirrel Chaser is fun to be around and this fun-loving spirit can make the trip enjoyable, but they can block progress. The next new shiny thing distracts them. Each new exit is a potential adventure. If you don't get distracted with them and follow their every whim, they can take it personally.

Personality 7: The Jerk

Mode of operation: "Loud and in front."

They can't stand to see everyone going in the "wrong" direction. But it's only their personal version of "wrong" because they think they know best. They will burnout themselves and others while they keep barking orders and saying, "One more mile".

Personality 8: Chicken Little

Mode of operation: "Screams "danger" at the shadows."

The sky is always falling. The past was awesome. The future is scary. The present part of the road trip is overshadowed with "we've never gone this way before".

The winter is a wonderful moment to get an honest look in the mirror. Once you see clearly you'll be eager to leave winter, but it's not over.

Action #2: Settle in. This is gonna take a while and it's gonna hurt.

The winter's gift is not only to teach you where you self-sabotage but also for you to learn who you are apart from your circumstances. We discover that the existential fear of the fall isn't real. It feels real when you're threatened, afraid and insecure. But who you are is never threatened. Your dignity, your very identity, is never on the line. Take a deep dive with me for a moment. You are more than roles you fulfill. You are more than the circumstances you experience. Your trials and failures do not define you. In the stress of winter you don't have to fall back on past accomplishments or dwell on past disappointments. You don't have to be down on yourself or proud of yourself based on whether you're doing a good job or bad job.

The fall wasn't punishment; it helped restore us by taking us to the bitter cold of winter where we get the necessary insight we need. The cold wakes us up, without which we would still be stuck and numb. The winter shows us the ineffective hustle and when that gets stripped away we can start to learn who we really are.

The gift of the winter is deeper insight. We learn we're not defined by the stuck points of fall. We study the past without being defined by it. When we separate who we are from what we do, we change how we process life. We look at the process more than the results. This allows us to strengthen our perseverance to follow our insights. We relax into the insights gained from the studying and listening to the winter and go wherever the truth of those insights may lead us.

I believe our truth is always blocked by shame and fear. The winter guides us to the truth of who we are. The winter is our sherpa as we walk along the jagged cliff's edge. The pain of the winter is our freedom. The fear of being judged and misunderstood by others starts to lose some of its sting and power. The shame of letting others down loosens its grip. Only at this point can what we truly desire come to the surface so that those desires may guide us into the action of spring. The most difficult part of this moment in the winter is when we have to let go of a reality that may never happen. All dreams don't come true. Some limitations are real and some barriers may not be broken anytime in the near future. Without the mourning of what may never be and the ashes of dreams that have died there can be no creative rebirth in the spring.

M. Scott Peck says it this way, "The truth is that our finest moments are most likely to occur when we are feeling deeply uncomfortable, unhappy or unfulfilled for it is only in such moments propelled by our discomfort that we are likely to step out of our ruts and start searching for different ways or truer answers." If our fall season is our rut, then our winter season is when we search for a different way or a truer answer to our issue.

We aren't ready for spring when we have our truer answer. Winter is still finishing its process in us. We have to deepen our resolve in the winter so we can see our spring through to completion. How do we deepen our resolve in the winter? We persevere and then persevere again.

I have explained the second action is to settle in for the insight that is to come. There will be moments when you want to quit, but I know you're going to persevere. You'll be ready for the winter to pass when you are armed with the new self-knowledge and empowerment you feel. You'll feel so sure that now is the midnight moment of the darkest darkness. Convinced that now is the very moment it's all going to change, you will assume the light is ready to break through. It will. But not yet. Winter isn't finished. Once you've endured, prepare to endure again. The fullness of your resolve hasn't been tested in whatever part of your life that you're done with the winter. This is why you need action number three.

Action #3: Remind yourself of the difficult times you've made it through.

The winter is training time for your mental resilience. It builds your grit. Say it with me, "I can do difficult things." You can. You already have.

Let's walk through it together. Look at the top five difficult things from your past that you have accomplished. This is proof that you have won in the past. Made it through the loss of your grandparents as a child? That was painful. Endured your parents' divorce? That was challenging. Did you put yourself through school? Are you raising kids as a single parent? Heck, if you've given birth you're a warrior.

I've seen it happen three times. I remember being so intensely involved in my first daughter's birth that as I was encouraging my wife to push, I was physically pushing until I was red in the face. The doctor gave me a concerned look as she warned me "Chris, if you keep pushing that hard you're going to give yourself a hernia." Side note: the highlight of that day, as you can imagine, was that my wife was elated for me to be at the center of attention during her delivery. See, I did a really hard thing that day.

This birth isn't limited to physical children. Birthed a vision for a business? Pursued an adoption? Started your life over in a new city without friends or family to support you? Fired your "c" level clients to work with those you enjoy serving? Stopped and kissed your partner goodbye when you left the house for work after you two had a fight? Hi, my name is Chris. I have done difficult things. You have, too.

Now, analyze your current winter moment. We need to build a bridge from past moments into our current winter situation. The same skills that we used successfully in the past will continue to help us today.

A few years ago when I ventured out to do this work full time, I faced a number of challenges. The preeminent challenge was I needed to make in one month what the business had produced the previous year. At the same time, I was committed to not pressuring people into sales or burning any bridges. I wanted people to have a life changing experience they felt invited into, not an experience that an arm twist convinced them they needed. I had a crazy goal to start a business helping others become effective and more human in their leadership that would spread to others. This was going to be difficult. I had to access my past.

In the 9th grade, I had started my first business making necklaces. In high school, I was placed into multiple leadership roles without seeking them out. During college, I had helped start a movement on campus that was never orchestrated but ended up involving over a hundred students. In each of these, I had already done what I wanted to do in part. I wanted to have a business that helped people lead their lives with awareness who would in turn share their growth with others.

Not only do we access our past for the present moments we want to advance, we also access our past to turn around deeply challenging circumstances. When we take ownership of our lives, we start building skills that will help us recognize more quickly the negative repeating patterns that are blocking our way. The same poor decisions and reactions that tripped us up before will repeat themselves unless we consciously take steps to change them. Until we learn to recognize the patterns of our story, we will live out the same story over and over. I know that on the surface our current winter situation may look completely different from the past difficult moments that you endured. I believe the current struggle you're facing can be endured with drawing on a skill or attitude that you successfully used in the past. You just have to find the connecting pattern.*

Sometimes the winter hits hard even if it's just a discouraging moment or specific situation. Other times winter hits long and you lose sight of the fact that spring is coming. Either way, it is normal to need someone else to remind you, "You're not crazy. It's going to be ok. You've got what it takes." To know you are in a winter is to recognize a moment you can ask for what you need and allow others to give you the gift of being seen, heard, and felt. You may find as you talk through your winter problem a spring solution emerges.

The people that are stuck in or avoiding winter don't learn the contours of the valley floor. They live on the hype of the fall season or the increased intensity of the winter season until they push everyone away. Get on your belly. Study your past and your current situation. Crawl through the valley and feel the rocks underneath you. You'll be running up the next mountain soon, but right now is the time to understand where you are and why you are there.

Happiness isn't some far off destination. It's knowing who you are in the midst of circumstances that don't make sense and learning how to bring the unobstructed expression of who you are into all you do. The result is a mission with laser-focused clarity. This mission is no longer what you think your mission needs to be to feel good about yourself.

At age 17, I had no map for my life. At age 18, I was convinced I had the complete map for my entire life. I had studied the trajectory of others and copied their maps. I decided where I needed to be at certain ages to hit benchmarks others deemed important. Then suddenly at age 30, that map died. A set of devastating circumstances helped me realize I had built my map on a false reality. My fall season was a wake up call. My winter season was long and desolate; however, a new map was born. I will turn 40 the year this book is published. I like my current map. It's one I've made for myself without trying to copy anyone else's map. I've learned how to become a mapmaker. I might make another map in my 50's. Who knows?

Give yourself permission to let go of any picture you have of your future self. If you were a child of the 40's or the 80's just because you told the world you wanted to be a lion tamer doesn't mean you have to stay stubbornly committed to that path. RIP Barnum and Bailey's. As a child you thought it would be cool to tame lions, but now you won't participate in their subjugation. You couldn't help it that your romanticized view of the circus hadn't evolved to not participate in the mistreatment of animals. The winter is your moment to welcome any reimagining that is necessary for your growth. The winter has something for you and you have one job: find it.

In a fall season, looking at someone else's map was dangerous because most of us were desperate to keep doing what was easy. Figuring out our own maps was too scary and too difficult. In the winter season, we begin to be confident enough to observe others without trying to fit into their mold. We give ourselves permission to become mapmakers. We make a new map as we gently erase where we dreamed we would be to accurately reflect where we actually find ourselves today. With our new map in hand, we forge ahead with new vision.

To make and to follow your own map requires a state of "seeing" most people never develop. The winter tests will grind you down and sharpen your resolve so you can see the far off land or vision you have for your future. Winter also teaches you to never lose sight of your peripheral vision. The winter helps you get a picture of your future to focus on while you also learn to stay engaged in the present of your peripheral moments. You're zeroed in and noticing what happens while you journey to that future. You are future focused and present engaged. No more frantic activity, ineffective hustle and making the leaks of your life worse. It's time to move with sharp, purposeful action.

We are now ready for the external activity of spring.

This pattern recognition is what I focus on in figurethatshiftout.com

CHAPTER 4:
SPRING

As you may remember I have some seriously mad basketball skills. Let's say I decided to try out for the recreation league at my local rec center. Before tryouts, I would need to spend time perfecting my shot. After months of dedicated practice, I would invite you to meet me at the gym so you could see my improvements. I would warn you in advance that I've spent every free moment practicing and perfecting my shot. I put in my 10,000 hours. As we warm up you notice that every time I shoot, I take a granny shot. In dismay you ask, "Have you really spent thousands of hours perfecting a granny shot? That was a waste of time and energy. Your shot is going to be blocked every time."

Routine>Intentions

As we emerge from the winter season into the spring season, we find a guiding truth: Routines trump intentions. Routines matter. And routines are the practices that make our intentions a reality.

We can intend to take the stuck places of our lives and improve them; however, intentions will not see us through. We need routines built on our intentions. We need to make sure they are the *correct* routines. An awesome granny shot won't help us accomplish our hoop dreams or life goals.

GOING BACK TO WINTER

The reason we need to review winter is because it is tempting to skip the internal work and move immediately to action. The need to impress people and always look busy is a hard habit to break. In winter we learned not to chase constant motion and hope to stumble on a win. As a kid, I remember sitting on a carnival ride in a chair that went around in circles while the entire platform spun around at a different speed and angle. I refuse to get onto those amusement rides today because I know that spinning around in circles will cause me to throw up. That is how I want us to imagine what skipping winter and starting the spring season too early will look and feel like. If we skip winter, we will eventually realize we are still stuck going around and around in circles. We will not reach our destination and we might back ourselves into a corner that makes us want to throw up. If we miss the transition from the winter to the spring, we will not be focused on the next action to take.

How can we tell if we skipped the winter season of a problem? We know we're forcing an early spring when we are distracting ourselves with busyness and relying on old solutions or routines. Or we might hatch a wild scheme that isn't actually in alignment with who we are. Wild schemes are great if they are an overflow of who we are.

I remember one winter season where I needed to rebuild my income. Rather than sit in the winter and take action with what was growing in me with the work I now do called SightShift, I got distracted with a plan for some quick money through a network marketing scheme. I say that in a whispered and embarrassed tone. I had a killer URL. I had yard signs. I put together a mini-radio campaign. I had a batch of leads I was cold calling. Natural gas was being made available in multiple states at a lock-in rate. I know you're twinging. Me, too. Looking back, I could have used that time and energy so much more effectively, but I was grasping at straws. At almost the same time, fracking began and natural gas prices dropped and the market for my product evaporated. Some people will say, "Hey, you got a tax write off." I would push back with one protest to wake you up. You can't write off wasted time and energy.

When we are panicked the best routine or action can elude us. Frantically grasping at anything, we might fall back into old habits and reactions or trick ourselves.

46

Even as you read this you may feel overwhelmed and defeated but it's not too late. We learn to cooperate with the season we are in. If we don't learn to accept our reality, we will miss gaining the discoveries that will take us to spring. Leaving some of our big questions unexplored means more trouble later.

There are 3 actions that spring wants to teach us.

Action #1: Surrender. And then surrender some more.

We are never finished surrendering. There are resources in us that we can't tap into until we grieve and let go. To grieve and let go, we have to surrender what needs to be released. We discover we have to surrender again and again at the very moment we feel drawn to the familiar path that catches our eye in the hard season. We surrender when we would rather numb out than continue the journey in the spring season. We surrender the climb. We surrender our focus. We surrender our pursuit. We continue refining it at every bend of the road when we ask ourselves the tough questions. In the winter season, we learned to grieve the past and our present in order to reimagine a different future.

Our different future can only begin after we grieve the ending. If we are going to experience a true, non-hyped new beginning, it will only come after we release old dreams and destinations. In the spring season, we've fully owned that we can't bring back old motivations. We find a new rhythm, a new motivation. Any spring season will require us to continually surrender being attached to a certain path. We need to be open to continual refinement. Continual surrender is the new action of the spring. We loosen our grip on the methods to conserve our strength for tightening our grip on the mission.

Moving forward in the spring, we need stay on the lookout for key distractions.

Action #2: Stop being distracted with busyness.

Busyness is practicing wrong. Busyness is wasting the energy the spring gives us. Busyness is reactively answering all your email rather than proactively setting up a meeting, staying up to date on social media rather than posting your vulnerable stories, or critiquing the works of others while failing to write the book that is in you. Busyness is organizing the files on your computer rather than building a new skill that will take you forward.

The incorrect action in the spring is trying to get our ducks in a row. We trick ourselves into staying busy chasing paths that will not lead us to our destination. We distract ourselves with good actions instead of the best actions. We distract ourselves from accomplishing what really matters. I remember when I had a dissertation that required a re-write. I avoided my desk for months. On the first day that I sat down to begin writing, my eyes were drawn to the disorganized bookshelf behind me. I had an urge to walk away from the pressure of finishing my dissertation by mindlessly organizing the books on my bookshelf. The last thing I needed to do was distract myself with busy work.

Once we walk away from propping up old motivations or blindly following some one else's map, we are motivated to make the best decision and take the best action. Our new inspiration produces an idea, an innovation or opens our eyes to a better path. Desire and hard work isn't enough. We have to make sure our actions are getting smarter. The winter evolves us. The winter season evolves the intelligence of our actions.

Action #3: Start practicing right.

Commit to small repeatable actions that are the result of your surrender and evolution. Rejecting busyness will free up your time and energy to start the action that will make the biggest difference. Do you remember my pesky dissertation that I avoided in my winter season? I needed to start writing using a spring season action. I decided to write for two hours that day rather than straightening up my bookshelves. Then I committed myself to write for two hours each day until the dissertation was complete. I finished my dissertation. Two years later I gave my library away. Any time I would have spent organizing those books would have been wasted.

The skill we develop in the spring is focus. A tree spends its energy and nutrients focused on creating buds. A tree has one job in the spring: grow. Your one job in the spring is to take action. Take the correct action. Then continue to take the correct action each and every day. We experience the effects of compound interest when we realize small, consistent actions can create dramatic change.

MAKING MEANING

A key result of the spring season is that you learn to make your own meaning out of your actions. Committing to small, repeatable actions might make us feel a little bored. Connect your practice to the bigger vision. This is how our life changes. We work the fundamentals. Maybe we consistently practice writing and telling stories to developing ourselves as public storytellers. Perhaps it is pushing ourselves to learn new models for team building so that we can draw on these skills to set us apart as leaders.

I believe your best is in front of you, but there is no shortcut to it. This is why a lot of people never go through dynamic and empowering change. The old attitudes, goals, and ways of responding to problems no longer work. That season is over. The old wrong actions are not what we need for the future. The future belongs to those who don't depend on others to make meaning for them but learn to make it for themselves.

Making your own meaning is making your own map. You seize courage to take a path that is yours. You have the opportunity to interpret your life free of the bias of others. Turning down that job offer might seem foolish to a loved one, but you know the wrong job will probably keep you from your future.

When you take insight from winter into spring, your next steps will result in actions that will make you feel vulnerable and exposed. As these larger projects or new insights push you beyond your comfort zone into your future, have the courage to stay on your path. Holding on to the meaning or vision of your repeatable actions will give you courage to move forward.

Staying encouraged to keep moving forward is a learnable skill. We take the surge of energy in the spring and we make rituals for ourselves. Rituals or practices or routines help signal our new reality. It's normal to feel like a fraud as we make changes.

When I started running a few years ago there were days that I would feel like a fraud if I missed a run. I may have already run 100 miles that month but the morning I missed one I could hear this whisper, "You're not really a runner." The winter helped us learn we aren't defined by what we do. I am Chris. I run sometimes. Whether I run or don't run doesn't matter. The spring is the time we pursue activity that came out of our winter insights. So whether it's deep meaningful routines like journaling or the simple morning routine of drinking two glasses of water a day, find ways to signal what is changing. Wake up what was stuck. Don't be afraid to create your own more elaborate rituals. Sadly we live in a world starving for the activity of spring and devoid of rituals that signal deep change.

We make graduating high school the signal of transitioning to adulthood when deep down we know memorizing information and learning to take a standardized test doesn't prepare you for adulthood. This is why people keep celebrating more and more graduations. It's the only ritual we know. First it was kindergarten, then 6th grade, and then 9th grade. At this rate every year will have it's own celebration. This is sloppy; however, it will entertain me to watch the de-evolution of our species as parents start to throw "walking" parties. "Come celebrate our child can walk five steps."

Often, we wait on someone else's affirmation to let us know that we have made it. "Son, you're a man." It might be the times we search our employer's eye to see a nod of affirmation or when we are desperate to hear, "Great job on the presentation." From small to big moments, we allow others to be the meaning maker for our lives rather than making our own. The winter has forged us to take who we are into spring and make our own meaning.

In the spring season, we use what we learned in fall and winter to pinpoint the passion in us and become laser sharp with our actions. We can use our spring energy in one of two ways: develop our skills or squander this moment. We also need to remember that staying busy for activity's sake will keep us stuck and cause us to miss the best moves forward.

Do I want to be "Dr. Granny Shot" or do I want to move forward?

Those of us who develop these spring season skills will get to enjoy the summer. Beach vacations don't pay for themselves.

CHAPTER 5:
SUMMER

The summer season is when we rest and learn to celebrate what we've accomplished. We relax in the moment. That's exactly what I was doing one summer as a passenger in a hot air balloon race. I was enjoying the summer day flying along, taking in the view, floating high above the world and all of its problems, when the pilot shouted, "Grab a post. We are going down." In an instant, our carefree, relaxed day turned to panic. A wind gust was forcing our balloon down and we began falling out of the sky. Our basket hit the ground and the wind drug the balloon basket through a field until we finally came to a stop.

This story illustrates why the summer season is so tricky and counterintuitive. We enter the summer season after we consistently took the best action on the best path and arrived at our destination. We look around, take a deep breath and feel a sense of "ah" that we did it! Most of us thought once when we achieved our goals and 'made it' that our problems would be over. Many of us thought once we clinched the championship, fell in love, took over the company, led the team, were elected into office or graduated with the coveted degree that we would have it made. As we look back over our lives, we see that even though we achieved certain goals, life continued to challenge, surprise, and change all around us.

There are two distinct ways we can fail the summer season: we become lazy or we fail to enjoy the summer. If we become lazy, we celebrate and kick back a little too much and fail to repeat the activity of the spring that brought us into summer. We rest. We play. Then, we rest and play some more. This path is dangerous because we take our eyes off the foundation.

The foundation begins to crumble when we stop taking the core actions and following the core practices that helped us succeed. We fail to be vigilant. Forgetting to be vigilant in the summer puts us at risk for losing our hard fought victories because our past successes will not be enough to keep us propped up for years to come. Did you ever wonder how someone making millions of dollars and enjoying the accolades of success could become bankrupt and broken? One hit wonders happen all the time. They became lazy. Maybe they became distracted. Or the calm of the summer allowed the old negative mindsets from their past to come to the surface.

We can also miss the opportunity to enjoy the summer. This is the other way we fail the summer and stay stuck. Never being content, never accepting good enough, and always wanting more is often lauded as a successful mindset. Instead of learning to breathe in and enjoy this moment for what it is, we keep chasing the need for more to soothe us.

Summer is difficult for ambitious performers. We can get addicted to needing chaos to stay engaged. We may struggle to enjoy a summer season if we always need another crisis to get us amped up. We need a crisis to keep us engaged. We need drama to maintain our attention. We enjoy being known as the person who swoops in and always saves the day.

Your leader may complain about having to fight fires to save the company while there's a lit match behind their back.

This environment will wear us out over the long term because there is never an opportunity to take a breath, celebrate the win, or enjoy the moment. A tree doesn't spend its summer season trying to produce multiple types of fruit to impress people who will visit the orchard. Constantly striving for more can keep us stuck in the summer season.

One of the most dangerous mental activities that blocks the enjoyment of our summer is comparison. Whether the comparison is to others or our own preconceived ideas we have an image of how we think life should look or feel once we have "arrived". There is almost always a gap in how we imagined it would feel and how it actually feels when we reach our destination. I remember moving into a custom-built dream home and questioning, "This is all the feeling of satisfaction I get for this?"

Rather than enjoy our summer we wait for the world to notice us and to celebrate us. This means many of us are clearing our throats louder and louder hoping the world will look up from their lives to notice ours. We're like children on Halloween, worried about what others think of our costumes, never realizing they don't notice ours because they are worried about their own costume. Not surprisingly we often delay enjoying our summer season while we are waiting for others to acknowledge and celebrate us. Until we receive the nod of recognition from the person we want most to impress or the person we really want to prove wrong, we can stay stuck.

Stop waiting for someone to give you permission to enjoy your summer season.

Summer is a time to refill our tank, unwind and relearn how to enjoy what has been accomplished. We want to move through summer by relaxing and playing while we keep an eye on our foundation.

Here's what it looks like: A CEO has achieved success beyond her wildest dreams. She stayed on her path and made it to her destination. There are new dreams and ideas already on the table, but she takes a moment before launching a new campaign to spend quality time with her family. They spend weeks planning a vacation with each family member having a voice. They decide to travel to an exotic location for a two-week getaway to recharge and strengthen their connection as a family. Every morning of vacation, she wakes up before anyone else to read over reports that came into the home office and glance over the accounts and ledgers. Then she and her husband have coffee on the patio so they can enjoy a quiet moment while their kids are still sleeping.

One morning her husband takes the kids to the splash pool by himself since she has an important conference call with a foreign company. No one feels cheated or ignored because it had already been discussed. The following day she will spend her time relaxing and focusing on her children while her husband goes on an exciting scuba dive on the reef wall. She has learned how to stay vigilant with the core practices that helped her succeed while enjoying the people around her. She knows that when she returns work will provide challenges and surprises as expanding into foreign markets will put her into a fall season in her work life, again. Instead of dreading the changes or pretending that life will always remain smooth, she drinks in this time and savors her vacation, her summer season.

Impact > Impress

Let's walk through some practices and actions that will help us engage in a healthy summer season. To frame these actions we must welcome the idea that the summer season is about becoming more of who you already are. It is normal to look back on insights gained from the winter and feel embarrassed by previous beliefs and actions. We utter, "I can't believe I did that." You don't have to look at your winter with shame or embarrassment. You've been on a journey to discover who you are and who you are becoming. The parts of you that you're embarrassed by need to be reconciled into the whole of who you are. All the knots and cuts in your tree trunk are a part of your story. If you don't make peace with the parts that embarrass you, you will posture yourself to impress others.

I wish I could I have a chat with you in person right now. I would ask you what you feel embarrassed by from your past. Then I would help you build a new relationship to that part of you as you understand you don't have to be embarrassed. That part of you is good and beautiful and powerful. It was just misdirected. Those mis-directions get corrected in the insight of the winter. As we relax into the summer, this isn't the moment to look back on those mis-directions with disdain. Look underneath for the good that is there. If we don't then we'll worry about what others think of our fall and winter seasons. When you are focused on the impression you're making, you risk missing the fullness of your ability to make an impact. Three actions will help you make the most of your newfound momentum while you stay true to who you are.

Action #1: Go back to the mission.

We take time to remember the why of our mission. We remember who we are and what we discovered in the winter season. Our future methods will change but our mission stays the same. In the fall season, we let go of false hype. In the winter season, we deepened our values and gained clarity. In the spring season, we sharpened our method and executed new plans on our path to reach our destination. While we are in the summer season, we restore the fire that motivated us to make it this far. We stoke the fire in the summer so we can confidently face our next challenge. Knowing the summer season won't last forever, we build ourselves up to prepare for the future. We reaffirm that we are committed to the mission, but acknowledge that how we get to our destination is open to change. Focusing on our mission reminds us to pay attention to the key places, the indicators, which let us know if we are on track, growing and healthy.

Most leaders, left to their natural insecure tendencies, tend to be better as a peacetime leader or a wartime leader. Depending on their bent, the insecure peacetime leader needs to live in a perpetual state of chill and falsely think being vigilant about anything is to be stressed. Or the insecure wartime leader lives in a perpetual state of hyper-vigilance. Frantically moving from one moment to the next, they treat all situations with the same level of urgency. Winston Churchill is known for leading brilliantly in wartime, however he struggled in his leadership as the country was ready to enjoy the peacetime he helped them achieve. If he had been able to appreciate his season, Churchill could have changed his approach. All leaders will lead in moments of peace and war. The summer is a moment to embrace the peace without losing the cautious eye towards the horizon.

Action #2: Evaluate what you are running to.

Closely examining where you are running to helps us pinpoint what is motivating us forward. It is a fresh awareness of what desires and dreams may have changed and determining if our destination may be slightly different or completely different than it was in the fall season. This is the time we ask ourselves, "Do I still care about this mission? Is it the same mission or has it changed as I've grown?" We might reengage in old dreams, but this time with fresh motivation. Instead of staying on the same path out of habit, we reevaluate the path to our desired destination. Does it need to change or could a minor tweak help catapult us toward our goal faster? This honest evaluation is designed to energize us and solidify our belief in our destination to help us run through future seasons.

Sometimes in a summer season we allow false reasons to keep us from the boldness of running into our pursuits whole heartedly and consistently. Your life will be determined more by what you do everyday than a few hyped moments of resolve. Summer is a great time to evaluate and decide where am I going to take the next courageous step?

Most of us can't initially identify the false reasoning that is keeping us stuck. Read through some of these and determine which one is keeping you from making the most of your summer season.

"If others would appreciate me, then I could engage in this moment." We will never receive enough validation and applause to make us always feel appreciated. No amount of awards or pats on the back can make us feel whole until we learn to appreciate ourselves and know we are secure. This might be us if we have every award and certificate we've ever won crowding the walls and bookshelves of our office. I once coached a guy whose company gave out applause boxes with "good job" stickers to all the employees to make the employees feel appreciated. How long will the clapping keep us engaged? If we need to open a box to hear people cheering, we are not engaging in a summer season.

"If I could feel accomplished enough, then I could enjoy this summer season." Chasing more keeps us from relaxing in the summer. We will never be accomplished enough. Life is always changing. New adventures are around every corner. Maxing out our bonus at work one year will not guarantee we will hit all of our numbers the following year. How much of our life are we willing to give away so we can feel good enough to someday relax in our summer season?

"I'll will enjoy the summer when I resolve all the issues around me." Refusing to enjoy our life, our summer season punishes us and everyone around us. Our desire to fix everyone else makes us the final authority on everything and usually very bitter. We've felt the sting of shame when someone looks at our life, our careers, or our decisions and says, "I can't believe you are doing that. I would never do that. What were you thinking?" Criticizing everyone around us makes us feel superior because it distracts us from our own internal voice that constantly shames us.

We know these voices in our head aren't true, but we still hear them so let's face them together. We know everything will never be perfect. It can be good. It can be enough. It will never be perfect. How will you speak back to your voice? If you feel you can't relax until it's all taken care of then ask yourself, "When is it all ever taken care of?" If you could solve all your problems, you would wake up with new ones. Recognize the false reasoning when you feel you can't enjoy the summer until everything is like you want it to be. Then enjoy running down the beach of your pursuits in your summer. You can't be at your best when you play in the summer season with an inner tension of conflicting voices. These unresolved voices will sap your mental energy.

Seasons are not static, they are dynamic. Postponing happiness until we are 100% secure puts us at risk of waking up the morning after our retirement party feeling a sense of loss because we never enjoyed a summer season of life. Sometimes our desire to plan for every possible surprise that life throws at us causes us to miss our summer, our party. We will never resolve all the issues since fixing one issue instantly changes the trajectory of another issue. Things around us are always changing. Even with the changes, we learn to enjoy the season for what it is and celebrate the win. By celebrating and throwing our own party, we own the win in our summer season. We build a foundation of confidence and success that will support us when we run into the next challenge in our lives.

Action #3: Expect surprises.

The third action we take in the summer season is to expect surprises. We set ourselves up for a misstep when we think we know exactly what the summer holds. It's easy to enjoy the feeling of success and growth, but we have to know in our core that change will come. Imagine a tree in the summer. It is soaking up the sun and drinking in the rainwater while providing shade and a fun place for children to climb and explore. Occasionally, a drought will cause the leaves to wither and die prematurely. Other times summers are memorable when excess rainwater pushes rivers and streams beyond their banks. During these summers, the rain soaked ground allows some trees to become uprooted. During the summer season, we pay attention to what seems to come out of nowhere because that will prepare us for the next transition into fall.

We know when we are missing a transition to the next season when we hold onto something that is no longer working. We continue propping up what used to work and keep trying to fit it into a new reality. Forcing an old habit will frustrate us and everyone around us when we fail to see that our summer season is over and we are transitioning into the fall season in one or more areas of our lives. Being consciously aware that we can be in the summer season at work and different seasons in other parts of our lives, we accept this and give each separate area of our lives what it needs. We may be in a winter season with our creativity and health but in a spring season with our spirituality and our finances. Each area of our lives has the potential to be in different seasons which means we can feel secure and insecure at the same time. Analyzing which seasons we are in sets us up for success when we give each separate area the actions and practices it needs.

What are the key metrics or measurements that let you know you're doing the best you can to make sure the foundation is solid? If we don't know what benchmarks and goals we are reaching towards, we never know when we are healthy and on track. We do this by asking ourselves what health markers and parameters will tell us when we are in a specific season or transitioning into a different season. Write these down so it's easy to quickly gain a visual of where we are winning and what areas need more attention.

I know I'm not vigilant with my business if I'm not exploring new ideas and having conversations with leaders as they work out their problems. If I don't know their pain, my words lose their effectiveness. I never want to be disconnected from the front line. I make sure those conversations are on my calendar. If I escape into the cave of book writing, some of my sharpness is dulled. When I work with leaders and they enter into a summer season I challenge them to think through the key actions that got them there so they don't stop repeating them.

I remember when a 70-year-old man I used to see in the sauna said to me, "All my friends who retired and then sat down are dead. I move and I use my mind. I meditate when standing in a line." What are the actions that keep you vigilant?

Our health is an area that we need to analyze since it is the easiest to ignore when life is challenging. Here are some questions you might put on your chart: Are our clothes too tight or too loose? Do we get winded when we walk up two flights of stairs? Glancing over the latest lab results will tell us if our body is struggling in a fall season. Spending a few moments thinking about the quality of our emotions will quickly give us clues to where we are and where we need to improve. Did we react with a level ten response to a level one trigger? Are we constantly angry and frustrated or relaxed and able to handle life's challenges?

What are the relational cues that we use to know if we are connecting with people we love? What were some of the benchmarks when you were dating? No, we aren't pretending that we have to fake the intensity of emotions and depth of attention we gave to a brand new dating relationship. We do not have to spend two hours primping for a date or splash on an entire bottle of cologne to have a strong, intimate relationship.

What we need to do is spend a few minutes remembering which key elements made the relationship special. Then we take the time and energy to reconnect with those we love in the best way for the people we are today, not the people we were years ago. What did the two of you do early in your dating relationship? Did you walk, hike, go to the movies, go to concerts or attend sporting events. Take time to add one of the activities onto both of your calendars and reconnect.

A reminder to help you navigate the summer season is a quote from one of the Batman movies. Bane reprimands Batman when he says, "Victory has defeated you." Batman became lazy in his summer. Don't become lazy in yours. Stay focused, keep your eyes on your foundation, relax and enjoy your season.

CHAPTER 6:
CAUTIONS

Glancing around my dinner table, I had the sudden realization that I no longer felt a sense of awe at being a dad. What once felt like a miracle had become mundane. That was over a year ago and it was something I never wanted to admit to myself, much less anyone else. Instead of stuffing those feelings down inside myself and pretending it wasn't true, I acknowledged the emotion even though it made me sad and uncomfortable. Realizing that if I didn't pay attention to those thoughts and lean in, I could become stuck with a loss of appreciation for one of my most important roles and never regain a sense of awe. That loss of appreciation would lead to at best ineffective parenting and at worst hurtful indifference. I didn't want to stay stuck for them and me. The desire to progress was so strong it outweighed the feeling of shame.

In between bites at the dinner table, yes, that is how fast a fall season can appear at the front door of any category of your life. One minute you are laughing and sharing stories while enjoying a delicious dinner with your family. The next minute you realize something isn't working. I didn't interrupt the dinner by standing up and declaring that I lost the wonder of being a dad. Entering a fall season doesn't need an announcement and it doesn't need someone to take the blame. I didn't need to put pressure on my kids to be good enough or loving enough to fix me. My kids, and possibly my wife, wouldn't hear that I was going through something, instead they might hear, "You are bad and not enough, so fix yourself to gain my love." In a fall season, we notice what is going on and decide to face it.

Realizing I've lost something puts me into a winter season of introspection and attention. I sat with the reality and owned that it was real. Even though it wasn't something I was proud of, I wasn't going to lie to myself. While I didn't schedule time on my calendar to overanalyze it, I noticed it and leaned in to the reality. I could have tried to skip the winter season with fake thoughts or pretending, but I didn't want to stay stuck. I wanted to learn what the winter had for me.

Six weeks later I was standing in line at a café talking to one of my favorite barista's. He makes the best fruity jack rose. I know some of you are thinking, "Emphasis on fruity," but you have to try it. I asked about his weekend and he shared how touching it was to watch his daughter play in the snow for the first time. I shared some advice someone gave me years ago, "You never know the last time something is going to happen. You never know the last time your children will ask you to comb their hair, read them a book, fill up their sippy cup, whatever." I immediately felt an intense sadness as I realized, I don't remember those last times. Without warning, I started to cry. Yep, I was that guy. Standing at the counter, I was in the winter season of grieving that my children were growing up and my role as a dad was changing. I stepped out of the way to allow the next person who wasn't walking through a winter season order their handmade delight. I'm wiping tears as I realize I am now in the "Over Shares with the Barista" group.

Just because I understood what was going on doesn't mean I was instantly transported into a spring season. I didn't immediately have new motivation and feel reenergized with the emotion of being a dad of little girls. What I noticed was a surge of energy to reengage with my children not as I had when they were children, but to engage fully as a dad of preteen and teenage daughters. I didn't think I would ever have to grieve them growing up, but I did. Now I can celebrate being the dad of older daughters as I relate to them differently and do not expect them to interact with me the same way they did in elementary school. I am in a summer season as I rest with where they are and continue to keep an eye on their changes and the ways our relationship will change as they enter high school, leave our home and start their own independent lives. (Or they can start paying me rent!) Things will change as they always do. For now, we are enjoying our summer season.

At some point, I will find myself in another fall season in some area of my life. It might be a relationship, a work situation, a financial situation or any other area of my life. Regardless of which areas need my attention, I will embrace the season for what it is. By facing it, I will keep it from making it more than it actually is and allowing it to become a stumbling block. I will acknowledge what I discover in the fall. I will sit with it in the cold of winter. I will wait for the inspiration of the spring season and then I will take the best action to enjoy the summer.

I wish everything clicked through the seasons in my life as clearly as it did with my awareness of being a father. It doesn't. You're going to go through some seasons for years in macro ways and some seasons in micro ways. In the smallest of moments of your day, you may move through the seasons quickly; however, you can stay stuck if you don't embrace your season.

And I've found paying attention to some cautions will help you as you make this journey many times.

WATCH OUT FOR THESE

Caution #1: You can't skip from fall to summer.

A lot of people want to skip a specific season. Whatever season they dislike the most is the one they will want to avoid. If they are afraid of the action of spring or the rest of summer they may want to stay in the winter. Emo kids anyone? I work with high performers who are willing to accept the fall season and recognize something isn't working; however, it is hard for them to sit still long enough in the winter to figure out what has really transpired. Running out of patience they will say, "I want to get back to how it was before." That's impossible for all of us. The winter is helping them get to the end of their patience. The sooner that happens the better.

You can't skip from fall to summer. If you try to hype yourself up to avoid the winter and spring season, you'll be skipping over the very first lesson we learn in the fall and that is truth beats hyped positivity.

I don't watch golf much unless I need an afternoon nap, but I've watched Tiger Woods go through losing his dad. From my viewpoint, he lost his connection to his golf game and has now spent years trying to force that motivation to come back. I'm not throwing stones. I just want to help him recognize the season. He needed to let go of the motivation that he was propping up so he can enter his winter season. Over time he could find a new motivation for golf, another sport, or a completely new, rewarding career.

As a kid I watched Michael Jordan do that with baseball. He left basketball for a bit and after trying his hand at baseball, he came back to basketball. He is also an amazing amateur golfer. Whether it's golf, basketball, being a parent, or work; motivations fade and pass. You can't prop up old ones. We release them and we await the arrival of the new motivation.

To protect you from Caution #1 let's go back to the tree. You are like the tree. You cannot control the seasons. You cooperate with them. You don't skip them. It might encourage you to remember that just because one area of your life is in the winter, it doesn't mean that has to color the view of your whole life. When one part of your life feels "off" resist the urge to make a blanket statement about your whole life. This prepares us to watch out for caution number two.

Caution #2: Our lives are made up of different seasons.

Most people want to make all of the pieces of their lives exist in their same favorite season. Life is complex. I could be in one season with my kids, another season with my wife, and another season with the business. I could take the business and break it down into five separate pieces and they could each be in a different season. Maybe sales are in one season but the team is in another. As people advance in leadership responsibilities and as they grow older, they often feel overwhelmed at the complexity of life so they treat every area like it's in the same season. Most people have a season that is their default season. If the summer season is their favorite, they just want to force everything to be chill and bury what they need to address. This is why adulting can be so difficult from the outside looking in.

Maybe the fall season is their favorite. They love the introspection and diving deep into what needs to be released. For other people winter is their favorite season and they crave the melancholy of sitting with all that needs to be released. For some, it's the hype of the new that has them skipping other seasons to search for the spring season.

Regardless of whatever season is most natural for you to embrace, please understand that you're going to have the most growth in your life by embracing the season you're most afraid of. Growth will come from whichever season you might say is your nemesis.

To protect yourself from this caution, learn to compartmentalize. I can have a fight with my wife before work and still lead a productive meeting that day. Compartmentalizing is unhealthy if you never return back to the moments of disarray or pain; however, it is healthy to not allow the moments of pain in one part of our life to dominate the other parts of our life. Healthy people aren't dominated by nor do they deny their emotions. They address what they can when they can as they can. Of course, that evening I made up with my wife as soon as I came home. Learning you are more than the roles you fulfill allows you to switch channels between the roles and be fully present in each moment.

That makes me think of a ukulele. One day I was walking down a sidewalk in between meetings feeling like a disappointment to my kids as their provider. My daughter had wanted to learn to play the ukulele. The desire was there and she was even practicing some songs like I do when I've turned up Soundgarden in the car and use my seat belt to wail the air guitar. Except, unlike me, she was actually practicing chords! We had already spent our extra money on another daughter's interest that week so we didn't have extra cash in our budget. It didn't matter what our budget was telling me, I just wanted to buy her a freaking ukulele. I felt weak in my role as a provider, but I had to remember that I am more than a provider. I was in between meetings and only had a few minutes to grieve the moment before I needed to show up and be fully present with the people I was leading. I remember thinking, "I am Chris. I fulfill many roles, but I am able to switch between those roles as needed." I wasn't defeated. I didn't have to feel devastated about my entire life because of what was happening in one area. No one's life is as solid as it looks. We all have places of struggle. I've learned to compartmentalize and not allow myself to get swept away by the wins or crushed by the losses. The following week I was able to surprise my daughter with a ukulele and maybe one day I'll post a video of her playing the ukulele. (If she even picks it up at all. Teenagers!) I'm so glad I didn't let hurt in one area dominate the other areas of my life. I'm also thankful that I didn't deny the hurt. I used the circumstance to teach me that whether good or bad is happening, no matter what season I am in, there is no circumstance that can take away nor add to my dignity. Some of the most painful moments of compartmentalizing my life do not belong in this book. When I share these more private painful moments while speaking or working with my coaching clients, they grasp how powerful it can be when you compartmentalize without ignoring the pain.

I know we're recovering from a leadership model that celebrated the ability to deny feelings and perform. The previous generation shut down desire to make their payments on time and ended up with a garage full of junk. At the same time, we don't want to swing to the other extreme of letting one area bleed into all the other parts of our lives in the name of authenticity. Being constantly distraught and inconsolable is equally broken. It isn't authentic leadership to bring baggage from one area of your life into another. It's immature. I can go to the pool with my kids or take a run when one part of my world is on fire and needing attention. Developing the ability to compartmentalize will allow you to refuel and re-engage the fire with a healthy and calm perspective.

Recognize the season you're in. Make the best decision you can for that season and then you don't have to force anything. If you do that, you will flow.

Caution #3: Friendships

If we're not careful, any friends that are staying stuck will pull us into their own seasonal stuckness. If our friends refuse to take the correct action to progress through their seasons, they will be frustrated. They may also endanger us by dulling our abilities to notice the critical actions for our own season. We become like the people we spend the most time with.

I'm not saying that we reject these friends, but without seasonal awareness we're going to let some of their bad habits rub off on us. Their stuckness might not look stuck on the outside. They are busily trying to make things happen with spring like energy. Unfortunately, they haven't sat in their winter to consider what is the most effective course of action. We think it's smart to be around them because of their get-it-done attitude and pace; however, we are in a fall season, needing to release something. Good friends will be growth oriented and support you in any season you find yourself. Good friends will also allow others to take the time they need to make the necessary and critical changes. If you live on a growth trajectory over time, you'll look up and any friends that stay perpetually stuck won't be around you.

IF YOU RESPOND WITH THESE YOU MISSED SOMETHING

When I had to rebuild my income with nothing in the bank I learned all this in a way that changed my life. At one point I was a substitute teacher and used my lunch breaks to study in the school's library for a degree I was close to completing. I realized I could hype myself to prove to the world I had what it takes. It's the make-it-happen-with-a-chip-on-my-shoulder approach that makes you fun to be around (he says sarcastically). I could hype myself to prove that I could make a comeback but all that proving energy would drain others and me over the long term. If I was going to come back from setbacks that had ruined the lives of so many others who had been in my position, I had to do it differently. I had to learn to show up everyday with nothing to prove.

Let me break down and answer some objections you might have right now:

"You don't know my situation. I have to stay hyper vigilant and answer emails late into the night." I know the pressure is real. I know the feeling of learning to go to sleep with bank accounts that will go negative while you sleep. You can anxiously toss and turn all night or learn to sleep under the pressure so you can wake up refreshed and make things happen the next day.

"You don't know the people I work with." Correct. I don't know them, but I know of them. There are patterns. Learn to cut your path and have them react to you rather than you reacting to them.

"I'm drowning in information and this feels like one more thing to do." We live in an age of too much information and not enough wisdom. Become your own best guide so you don't have to worry about consuming all the information. You'll be able to selectively grow where needed.

"I don't have any time to waste. I need to stay extremely aggressive with my pace a little while longer." A little while turns into a long time very quickly. Then, you've conditioned yourself to bury stress patterns and actually will have built negative triggers to keep you working in an anxious state.

"I need to get away for a long break." Maybe a break will help interrupt your pattern, but then you'll return to it as soon as you come back. The real challenge is to learn a relaxed mindset in the midst of the chaos. Monks in the desert can write books about being relaxed, but the real test is living relaxed in the stresses and demands of life.

"This will kind of work itself out someday." Nope. The bad habits and mindsets of others are dulling the sharpness of your impact. The vivid brilliance of your life fades. Reverse course immediately.

"I need more hustle and more discipline." If that were true, then more would do it every time. It takes courage to adopt new practices and beliefs.

"I don't like what you're saying or how you're saying it. I just want to watch motivational videos and hustle harder. I'll post videos of me working at 11:30 pm to prove how hard-core I am." Sure. Go for it. I'll be here when you're done wearing yourself out with that nonsense.

Don't you get tired of people trying to prove they are working hard? Ahem, just like I used to do. Hi, my name is Chris and I'm president of the Prover Club. I'm ready to step down and retire the gavel. I could call it "hustle" and make it sound like a rite of passage. But continually hyping yourself up will diminish your ability to draw on your internal motivation. Listen, no BS. I don't search for motivation. I unblock it within myself.

How? I have learned how to relax even when I don't think I have the time. I don't work myself to burnout. Hold up. Truth moment. I do still struggle with this when I'm excited about a big goal. I am facing the truth that at each new level of growth with business and family roles, I have to re-learn what it means to relax even when parts of my life are not in summer seasons. This helps me enjoy my journey for what it is. When I lose sight of this, I perform poorly as a human. I can be uptight, rigid, and intense. When that happens I try to redirect my attention. It can be a simple nap in the sun or going for a walk to feel the wind on my face. If you can't allow yourself to have fun, to relax, to enjoy moments in and out of work, then you'll never find the freedom you want. No matter how successful your business becomes or how many hours you put in to the weekly grind, the hamster wheel keeps spinning fruitlessly. If you believe you can't relax until you reach the fairytale destination of a perpetual summer, then do I what I did in my 20s when I felt bad if I wasn't constantly studying and learning. I look back on those moments and wish I had done more to stop and enjoy the season. Seasons are cyclical. Enough will never be enough if the goal is perpetual summer. Working smart by cooperating with your season and enjoying all your time is the real goal. You can be free of the lie that says relaxing is a luxury.

Conventional wisdom will pressure you. Pressure will activate you for the moment, but it won't teach you how to tap into your own guidance system. So figure out where you are. You're one shift away from relaxing into your brilliance. Embrace your season.

EPILOGUE

As we close, I want you to be aware of the breadth and depth of this model's applications. I find it's like breathing. We inhale the fall as we stir desire of what needs to change. Then, in the winter, we exhale as we sit with our reality. We inhale energy and new direction in the spring. In the summer we exhale the energy to rest. This awareness of breath helps me be mindful.

The depth of this seasonal pattern guides me further. Mindfulness isn't enough. I also need to develop my mindset. This seasonal model aids me to sharpen my mindset. In the fall season, I don't know what I don't know. I embrace the uncertainty. I am no longer superstitious. In the winter I stop tricking myself. I am no longer my own worst enemy. As the spring season begins, I get insight to what changes must be acted upon. I am no longer a victim.

In the summer I mature. My growth gives me gifts I can share with those around me. I am no longer egocentric.

From movies to literature to sacred journeys, the pattern remains the same. There's a time to let go, a time to introspect, a time to act, and a time to rest. As one ancient poem states, "There is a season for everything under the sun."

I use the seasons to give myself permission to not be dominated by emotions nor deny them, but allow them to guide, teach, and grow me. Each season contains a pressure to feel a certain way. In the fall we get stuck when we resist accepting reality. We emotionally identify with the failure, the setbacks, and the disappointments. We falsely believe they define us. To be stuck in the fall is to feel that your pain or stuckness defines you. To progress through the fall is to know that no circumstance is an attack on your dignity. You never have to surrender your dignity even when you admit something isn't working.

To be emotionally stuck in the winter is to believe frenetic activity will relieve your suffering. Frenetic, panicked attempts won't change your reality; it will only burn you out. Since you emotionally let go in the fall, you can brace yourself for what you will learn on the other side in the winter. The insight will be there. Sit with the pain. Study it. There's a sage within you ready to be awakened in the winter. The pain and chaos you want to run from is your emotional training. This training protects you from crumbling under future pressure.

Being emotionally stuck in the spring is to resist taking the action that will make you feel vulnerable. It's scary to try on new ways of relating, commit to new actions, or put yourself out there in vulnerable ways. You must go and attempt what your inspirations are whispering could be true of your life.

To be emotionally stuck in the summer is to rigidly protect your relaxation by not staying open for the next growth opportunity that will come. Fall will enter your life again.

Wherever you find yourself, I hope that you can embrace the fall and pay attention. Notice the pain and lean into the winter. Position yourself for change in the spring as the moment flips and then relax in the summer as you flow. You are the tree so be ready to start the process all over again. May you use the seasons to emotionally open new dimensions to who you are, capacities in your roles, and resilience in your pursuits.

SEASONS REFERENCE GUIDE: ACTIONS TO TAKE IN EACH SEASON

FALL:

Truth > Hyped Positivity

Accept reality.

Explore what I am avoiding.

Am I forcing old motivations in any area?

Discover what addictions or distractions are in my way.

Speak to what you are afraid of.

Notice what gets under my skin too quickly.

When do I react with a level ten response to a level two problem?

Notice where could there be a better result.

Admit where am I forcing something.

Learn how to let go of what isn't working.

Notice thoughts, actions, and their results at a deeper level.

Acknowledge areas I am avoiding reality through addictions.

Shed and release.

Realize I have been tricking myself about reality.

Realize I do not have as much control as I thought.

Learn about the difference between a path and a destination.

Acknowledge what isn't working.

WINTER:

Clarity>Intensity

Grieve what was lost or stolen.

Do you feel like you've reached the bottom or end of your motivation?

Discover what is embarrassing or what you are covering up.

Realize our trials and failures don't define us.

Stop doing what we've done out of habit or fear.

Remove distractions during this season.

Look for a rebirth.

Study yourself.

Train for the success. Train for failure.

Grant yourself permission to stop.

Recognize patterns.

Lean in, explore, and study the situation.

Learn to be present and pay attention.

Give compassion and acceptance to ourselves in the midst of our struggle.

Accept the gift of winter.

Remind ourselves of the difficult times we've made it through.

Remind ourselves that if one or more area of our lives is in winter we don't have to despair.

Compartmentalize in a healthy way.

SPRING:

Routines > Intentions

Projects move from "I need to" to "I want to".

Share an idea you're eager to process with a friend or business associate.

Where do I feel like the clouds parted on a solution to an existing problem?

Where do I need to be focused?

How am I distracting myself?

I need to stop the busyness that I am using to distract myself.

Discover which repeatable actions need to be taken consistently.

Decide what fundamentals need to be developed.

Create routines that will help me succeed.

Surrender.

Keep surrendering.

Embrace new motivations.

SUMMER:

Impact >Impress

Do I still care about this mission?

Is the mission the same or has it changed?

Is there a reason I'm refusing to celebrate?

Reject the lie that if I felt accomplished enough, then I could enjoy the moment.

Reject the behavior that I can only celebrate when I resolve all the issues around me.

Don't postpone happiness until everything is perfect.

Reconcile the parts of ourselves we are embarrassed by.

Authentically accept who we are.

Enjoy what has been accomplished.

Enjoy who you are.

Care more about impact than impressing people.

Restore the fire that motivated us to get where we are.

Go back to the mission.

Evaluate what you are running to.

Expect surprises.

Check indicators that we are on track, growing and healthy.

WANT TO KNOW MORE ABOUT
SIGHTSHIFT OR HAVING CHRIS WORK
WITH YOUR LEADERS?

SIGHTSHIFT.COM

SIGHTSHIFT ATHLETES HELPS ATHLETES
AND COACHES REMOVE DISTRACTIONS
AND RELAX WITH PRESSURE.

SIGHTSHIFTATHLETES.COM

**HYPE WEARS OFF.
PRETENDING IS EXHAUSTING.
NO MORE LEADERSHIP FADS.
YOU GLOW OR FADE.**

THIS IS FOR LEADERS, ENTREPRENEURS,
AND THE AMBITIOUS FREAKS.

FIGURETHATSHIFTOUT.COM

56166997R00059

Made in the USA
Columbia, SC
21 April 2019